Original title:
The Art of Being Creative

Copyright © 2024 Swan Charm Publishing
All rights reserved.

Editor: Jessica Elisabeth Luik
Author: Eliora Lumiste
ISBN HARDBACK: 978-9916-86-546-0
ISBN PAPERBACK: 978-9916-86-547-7

Inventive Realms

In realms where dreams and thoughts entwine,
Imagination's threads combine,
Crafting worlds both bold and bright,
A canvas vast of endless light.

From whispers of the ancient lore,
To futures never seen before,
An artist's brush, a writer's pen,
Their tales come to life again.

Mountains, oceans, skies so vast,
Moments captured, shadows cast,
Boundless journeys to be seen,
In the heart of forest green.

With each idea, horizons break,
New beginnings from thoughts we make,
A universe within the mind,
Infinite, unique, defined.

So venture to these realms unseen,
Where fantasies and truths convene,
Feel the magic in the air,
Inventive realms, beyond compare.

Saga of Spirits

In twilight's gentle, fleeting haze,
Where shadows softly intertwine,
Ancient spirits dance and gaze,
   Beyond the edge of time.

Whispers of forgotten lore,
Echo through the ageless night,
Guiding travelers evermore,
   Toward a realm of light.

Moonbeams carve a silver path,
Through forests dark and deep,
Harmonizing with the whispers,
   Of those who never sleep.

In this realm of dreams and sighs,
Where past and present blend,
Every spirit finds its skies,
   In stories without end.

Sea of Innovation

Beneath the dawn of endless blue,
A sea of dreams within our grasp,
Ideas like waves come surging through,
Breaking free from the past.

Horizons wide and unconfined,
Calling forth the brave of heart,
To navigate uncharted winds,
And play a visionary part.

Anchored minds now set adrift,
Innovations chart their course,
For every challenge, there's a gift,
A new and potent source.

In this sea of endless wonder,
The future takes its rightful place,
With minds as vast as skies of thunder,
Leading forth the human race.

Dreamer's Voyage

Beneath a tapestry of stars,
A dreamer casts their hope anew,
Set sail for realms both near and far,
On pillows made of dew.

Each wave a whispered lullaby,
Each breeze a tale untold,
As dreams evolve and amplify,
Into adventures bold.

Mountains rise to touch the skies,
Valleys whisper secrets deep,
Dreamer's heart in endless ties,
With visions they must keep.

With courage fierce and purpose grand,
Their journey finds its light,
On dreamer's voyage, hearts expand,
Through the velvet night.

Aesthetic Whispers

Silent musings paint the air,
In shades of dusk and dawn,
Aesthetic whispers softly share,
The magic they have drawn.

Brush of light on canvas vast,
A symphony of hues,
Every moment's fleeting cast,
A palette of the muse.

Nature's voice in silent flow,
Through petals, leaves, and streams,
Every whisper weaves a glow,
In the tapestry of dreams.

Beauty's song in quiet strains,
Echoes through the heart,
Aesthetic whispers, soft refrains,
In gentle art impart.

Visionary Beats

In drums of destiny, we march as one,
Through fields of dreams, the battles won.
A symphony of stars, our path so bright,
To the rhythm of hope, we take flight.

Echoes of future, in nights so still,
Whispers of fate, they guide our will.
Hearts entwined in cosmic grace,
Time unfolds, we find our place.

In shadows danced by firelight,
Visions bold, take hold of sight.
Bound by beats of ancient lore,
We forge ahead, our spirits soar.

Rhythms pulse through every vein,
In the quest for truth, we break the chain.
Unified in a visionary trance,
Step by step, we lead the dance.

As galaxies collide in cosmic glee,
We paint our dreams upon the sea.
In beats of love, and waves of peace,
The journey flows, a timeless piece.

Flights of Fancy

Beneath the clouds, we weave our tales,
On wings of wonder, truth prevails.
Imagination lifts us high,
Across the boundless, endless sky.

Dreamscapes form in twilight's glow,
Mystic winds begin to blow.
Through realms of thought, where visions gleam,
We journey far on feathered dream.

Stars alight on whispers bold,
Stories shimmer, yet untold.
In each flight, a voice anew,
Colorful, the world we view.

Minds align in cosmic flight,
A dance of ideas in the night.
Yet higher still, we dare to soar,
Unlocking secrets at our core.

In flights of fancy, freedom reigns,
A universe in vibrant strains.
Through the ether, pure delight,
We chase the dawn, we greet the night.

Phantasmic Expression

Through twilight's veil, illusions crawl,
A dance of shadows on the wall.
Phantoms form in spectral light,
To whisper secrets of the night.

Ink spills forth, in patterns vast,
Stories etched from futures past.
Thoughts take shape in boundless form,
A quiet calm before the storm.

In silent dreams, where echoes play,
Images float, then drift away.
On canvas dark, bright visions flash,
Moments caught in fleeting dash.

Spectral shades in phantom guise,
Come alive in poet's eyes.
In realms unseen, expression flows,
A dance of words that no one knows.

Phantasmic echoes, pure and wild,
Crafted worlds in moments mild.
In every line, a life unfurled,
A journey through the unseen world.

Creative Contours

In lines of light, our voices blend,
A canvas vast with no end.
Each stroke a whisper, soft and bright,
The dawn of dreams within the night.

Contours curve like rivers free,
Flowing forth in poetry.
A dance of lines, a symphony,
Crafted out of mystery.

Shapes emerge in colors grand,
Brushes held in artist's hand.
From heart to hand, the spirit flows,
In hues that only nature knows.

Creative contours, minds unleashed,
In every curve, a soul is reached.
Boundless forms in endless quest,
A masterpiece, the very best.

Through every stroke, a world is born,
New realities, the old forlorn.
In art, we find, a truth so pure,
Creative contours that endure.

Limitless Horizon

The sky expands in shades of blue,
Where dreams ascend, they break in two.
A world unhinged from doubts and fears,
Embracing suns and silent years.

Beyond the edge, where stars ignite,
A canvas broad with endless light.
Horizons stretch, no bounds to see,
In realms where hopes forever flee.

With every dawn, a new begun,
Horizons wait, igniting run.
Bound by naught, in shadow's grace,
Across the plains of boundless space.

We chase the winds, we hold the dawn,
In timeless fields, where dreams are drawn.
No fence to bind our spirit's flight,
In limitless horizon's light.

Ephemeral Sparks

In twilight's dance, the sparks do fly,
Ephemeral moments racing by.
A fleeting glimpse, a whispered touch,
In heart's embrace, it means so much.

Light ephemeral, it fades to dark,
Yet leaves behind a glowing mark.
Seconds stolen, yet so grand,
In temporal grip, we make our stand.

Swift they pass, these sparks of time,
In symphony, a fleeting rhyme.
Memories etched in golden frames,
Ephemeral dance, with whispered names.

Caught in moments, bright they shine,
Ephemeral sparks, forever thine.
Brief they are, yet grand and bright,
In fleeting dawn, they give us light.

Creative Convergence

Where minds collide in vibrant hue,
Creative sparks find paths anew.
In blended thoughts, ideas take flight,
Convergence brings the dark to light.

A symphony of varied skill,
Together shaping, bending will.
In union strong, creation soars,
Unlocking wide, uncharted doors.

The fusion forms a novel scheme,
A tapestry of vivid dream.
Converging paths lead futures clear,
In unity, no room for fear.

Bound in art, no limits seen,
Creative force forges the scene.
Convergence breeds a world so grand,
We shape the sky with one command.

Mindful Inventiveness

In quiet minds, new worlds are born,
With thoughts that break the darkest morn.
Inventiveness in whispers, soft,
Grows wings and takes our visions aloft.

Contemplative sparks do intertwine,
In spheres of silence, pure design.
Mindful motions, in waves they spread,
Creating life from visions in our head.

Imagination's silent sway,
Unveils new realms in break of day.
Invention rooted in the calm,
We find our song, our healing balm.

With mindful thought, we build anew,
Inventions bright, from visions few.
In stillness grows inventiveness,
A quiet force, a mind's caress.

Fantasy's Frontier

Beyond the veil of what we see,
Lies a land of mystery,
Where dreams and visions intertwine,
In realms where stars and moon align.

The echoes of a dragon's roar,
Rivers of gold from shore to shore,
Enchantments woven in the air,
Magic lives and lingers there.

Wanderers of time and space,
Find solace in this hidden place,
Whispers of an ancient lore,
Unlock the secrets held in store.

Across the fields where shadows dance,
Seek the path of happenchance,
In a world where myths are clear,
We embrace Fantasy's Frontier.

Unchained Mind

Thoughts like rivers, freely flow,
Unleashing dreams where few dare go,
Within the mind, an endless sky,
Ideas spread wings and learn to fly.

Chains that bind are cast away,
In realms of thought, we stray and sway,
Infinite paths before us wind,
In the vastness, our minds find.

Boundaries blur, and walls come down,
In the kingdom of the crown,
No borders hold, no limits fence,
The mind's domain is immense.

From a spark of endless grace,
Ideas emerge and interlace,
In every mind, a universe,
Unchained thoughts are our converse.

Creative Constellations

Through the night, the stars unfold,
Stories in the sky are told,
Each constellation, bright and bold,
A canvas vast, in starlight gold.

The night sky whispers, softly sings,
Of dreams and many wondrous things,
Creative visions come to life,
Amidst the stars, without strife.

Mapping paths with cosmic ink,
On the edge of dreams, we blink,
Imagination's sacred flight,
In constellations, burning bright.

Galactic trails, we leave behind,
In the tapestry, intertwined,
Our souls across the heavens dance,
In a cosmic, endless trance.

Awakening Possibilities

In dawn's first light, the world's anew,
A realm of possibilities in view,
The shadows part, the darkness fades,
As hope's bright beams our paths invade.

Through fields of dreams, we walk with grace,
New horizons we embrace,
Each step we take, with heart and mind,
Awakening worlds we've yet to find.

With every sunrise, courage grows,
In morning's light, our spirit shows,
Boundless potential in its glow,
Infinite seeds, we dare to sow.

From the night's embrace, we rise,
To greet the day with open eyes,
In the expanse of newfound day,
Awakening possibilities light our way.

Dreamsmith's Forge

In the heart of midnight's glow,
Where the stars in silence lie.
Smith of dreams begins to show,
Forging wonders in the sky.

A hammer shaped by moonlight,
Strikes an anvil of the night.
Creating visions pure and bright,
In a realm beyond our sight.

Sparks of fantasy ignite,
Melding truth with shimmering lore.
Every swing refines the light,
Casting forms we can adore.

Chasing shadows from the deep,
Waking thoughts from slumbered lore.
In the whisper of our sleep,
Ideas beam from dreamsmith's core.

Molded dreams rise and gleam,
In the fire of boundless craft.
From the forge of nights supreme,
Wonders fold in fate's own draft.

Whispered Brilliance

When silence veils the night,
Gentle whispers weave their thread.
Murmurs dancing out of sight,
Crafting thoughts within our head.

Softly hums the spark of light,
Illuminating shadows gone.
Brighten up the darkest plight,
Till the first hint of dawn.

Glimmers speak a silent truth,
Hidden deep within their glow.
Wisdom traced from ages youth,
Guiding hearts to bravely grow.

Cascading through the twilight veil,
Ideas whispered in the breeze.
Inspiration's subtle trail,
In the rustle of the trees.

Brilliance whispered, hushed and fine,
Illumines minds from realms unseen.
Through the echoes of time,
Dreams enkindle and serene.

Fleeting Genius

In a fleeting breath of time,
Glimpses of pure genius pass.
Flashes of thought, so sublime,
Mirror angels in their glass.

Moments' brilliance, quick and bright,
Ignites the soul's eternal flame.
Vanishing in morning light,
Gone before we know their name.

Spark of genius flickers fast,
As the seconds swiftly race.
Ephemeral yet vast,
Transcends the bounds of space.

Lightning bolts of pure insight,
Dissipate within our reach.
Epics written through the night,
Turn to whispers, memories teach.

In the swift and silent gleam,
Genius whispers, minds confess.
Fading like a wistful dream,
Leaves us humbled, none the less.

Thought's Winged Flight

In silent dawn, a whisper grows,
On wings of thought, it softly flows.
Across the sky, where day meets night,
Ideas soar in boundless flight.

Through realms of dreams, they lightly tread,
Unknown landscapes where they are led.
With every beat, they seek the light,
Imagination taking flight.

Higher still, where vistas spread,
Over clouds, where stars are shed.
Unseen horizons come in sight,
On thought's wings, in pure delight.

A journey vast, with trails unsown,
Explored by minds, by heart alone.
We chart the skies, we chase the bright,
On thought's winged flight, in endless height.

Radiant Possibilities

Where morning breaks with golden hues,
The world awakes with endless views.
Each ray of sun, a chance anew,
Radiant paths for dreams to pursue.

In fields of hope, where flowers spring,
Possibilities start to sing.
A symphony of what might be,
In every glint, in every tree.

Where shadows cast by doubt dissolve,
And hearts with courage start to evolve.
A tapestry of light and gleam,
Weaves bright the fabric of a dream.

Through tunnels dark, a piercing glow,
Guides each heart where they must go.
With rays that light both path and plea,
The world unfurls with what could be.

Innovation's Embrace

With sparks that light the sky anew,
Ideas blaze with vibrant hue.
In every thought, a seed is sown,
Innovation makes its home.

Beyond the realms of what we know,
Through endless mindscapes, we will go.
In unexplored terrain, we brace,
The unknown's bold, sweet embrace.

With every leap, a barrier breaks,
The future's form, our courage shapes.
A world transformed by daring hearts,
Innovation's spark imparts.

From smallest shift to grand design,
Creation's threads begin to twine.
In every turn, in every chase,
We find the path in innovation's grace.

Dreams in Bloom

In gardens lush, where thoughts take root,
Dreams unfold, to find pursuit.
Petals soft with morning dew,
Whispers of what might come true.

Beneath the sky, both vast and wide,
Hopes stretch tall, with arms spread wide.
From tiny seeds to full-treed plume,
Hearts and minds in dreams do bloom.

A tapestry of colors grand,
Weaving futures hand in hand.
Each dream a strand, in woven loom,
With endless hues in fragrant bloom.

The span of time, in sunlight's grace,
Nurtures every budding place.
In every heart, a vibrant room,
Where cherished dreams can softly bloom.

Infinite Reflections

Mirrors endless, light adores,
Shattered beams on mystic doors.
Fragments dance, a sparkling sea,
Echoes lost in reverie.

Time bends softly, whispers known,
In the realms where dreams have flown.
Glints of past and future blend,
Journeys through which hearts transcend.

Silent shadows weave and sow,
Canvas where our visions grow.
In this space, devoid of bounds,
Whispers weave their haunting sounds.

Labyrinth of lights entwine,
Soulful depths and thoughts combine.
Endless maze of mirrored hues,
Infinite, our path pursues.

Every step a mirrored flare,
Soul and mind in gentle pair.
Onward through the quiet night,
Seeking truth in silent light.

Muse in Motion

Dancing light on morning dew,
Whispers of the skies anew.
In your eyes, the world does spin,
Muse in motion, deep within.

Nimble feet on paths unknown,
Fetching tales from realms unshown.
Every gesture, pure delight,
Crafts a day from darkest night.

Flow of thought, like rivers fast,
Weaving futures from the past.
Sparkling eyes that hold the key,
Muse in motion, wild and free.

Gentle sway, the rhythm finds,
Seamless thread of kindred minds.
Steps that paint the patterns bright,
Waltzing dreams into the light.

Timeless dance where hopes entwine,
Boundless grace on which we dine.
In each move, a story sings,
Muse in motion, life it brings.

Symphony of Thought

Whispers soft in twilight's glow,
Echoes where our minds may flow.
Thoughts like symphonies arise,
In the realm where silence flies.

Notes we carve in shifting air,
Haunting melodies laid bare.
Memories, a fleeting song,
Played by yearnings lost and long.

Mindful chords that gently weep,
Through the valleys, shadows creep.
Harmony of dreams converge,
On the brink where thoughts emerge.

Waves of wonder blend and weave,
In the quiet, we perceive.
Every breath a minor key,
Tales of endless mystery.

Voices soft in silent night,
Threads of darkness laced with light.
In this symphony of thought,
Worlds unseen to life are brought.

Ocean of Creativity

Vast and deep, a boundless sea,
Waves of thought and mystery.
In the depths, where dreams reside,
Tides of hope and fear collide.

Currents flow with endless grace,
Charting realms of time and space.
Beneath the surface, wonders gleam,
Whispered secrets, silent scream.

In each drop, a world unfolds,
Tales forgotten, stories told.
Limitless, the ocean's span,
Crafting worlds within our hand.

Shores unseen, the mind explores,
Boundless depths and hidden floors.
Creativity's wild embrace,
Ever-changing, find your place.

Sailing through this aqueous plane,
Thoughts unbound, never tame.
In this ocean vast and free,
Lies the heart of what can be.

Dancing with Inspiration

In the silence of the night,
Whispers weave elusive light.
Dreams, they sway and softly call,
In the rhythm, we find it all.

With each step, a new spark flares,
Possibilities fill the air.
Twisting, turning, in a trance,
Creating space for chance's dance.

Listening close, inspiration sings,
Gifting us with unseen wings.
To ideas vast and wide,
Upon this dance, we glide.

Fleeting moments capture grace,
Traces left in time and space.
Echoes of a thought divine,
We dance with muse's twine.

As the dawn breaks through the dark,
We carry forward that bright spark.
Inspiration's endless flight,
Guides us through the night.

Inventive Horizons

Skies of blue and fields of green,
Threads of thought weave unseen.
Horizons stretch, inviting eyes,
Innovations softly rise.

From the earth, ideas grow,
Gently as a river's flow.
Boundless minds explore the sky,
Too daring to simply comply.

Journeys forged with heart and hand,
Across this ever-changing land.
To unknown realms, we voyage far,
Inventive dreams, our guiding star.

In the silence, notions bloom,
Filling the emptiness of the room.
Horizons painted with our minds,
In the unknown, purpose finds.

With each dawn, new worlds appear,
Possibilities crystal clear.
Inventive horizons gleam,
Embodying our shared dream.

Echoes of Originality

Within the heart of silence deep,
Original echoes never sleep.
Softly hum, a gentle song,
Where unique ideas belong.

In every shadow, light shall play,
Crafting fractals of the day.
Echoes whisper thoughts anew,
In the heart of me and you.

Unseen currents in the air,
Sing a chorus bold and fair.
Originality's pure grace,
Given breath and given space.

Through the labyrinth of time,
Echoes weave their silent rhyme.
Endless echoes, ever bright,
Original in their flight.

Beyond the dusk, beyond the dawn,
In every heart, they're drawn.
Echoes of originality,
Sing the song of infinity.

Visionary Paths

In the stillness of the mind,
Visionary paths we find.
Leading forth with steadfast grace,
Illuminating time and space.

Through the winding roads of thought,
Wonders sought and wonders brought.
Drawing lines in future's hand,
Pathways we can understand.

Every star a guiding light,
Through the deepest, darkest night.
Visionaries map the way,
To the break of dawn's new day.

Paths of promise, paths of hope,
Infinite in their scope.
Each step taken with pure sight,
Turning dreams into light.

On these paths, our spirits soar,
Ever seeking, evermore.
Visionary paths we tread,
Where inspiration's gently led.

Quantum of Creativity

In the realm where thoughts do gleam,
Particles of dreams ignite,
Ideas dance in quantum schemes,
Illuminating endless night.

Energy of minds entwined,
Synaptic sparks doth intertwine,
From chaos into forms designed,
Through boundless space, our spirits climb.

Waves of wonder, fields unknown,
Meander through the cosmic stream,
In every photon brightly shown,
New visions pulse within a beam.

Creation's thread, a silken thread,
Woven through the fabric grand,
Each fleeting thought, a needle led,
By unseen hands of wisdom's hand.

In the flux of time and space,
Where all dimensions intertwine,
Quantum states, a boundless place,
Unveil the truths by light defined.

Burst of Brilliance

A spark ignites, the mind's delight,
In darkness blooms a fierce light,
Bursting forth in radiant flight,
Transforming shadows into sight.

Epiphany in fleeting form,
Explosions of a golden storm,
From deep within the quiet norm,
A brilliance born, anew, transformed.

Each revelation, vivid bright,
In moments frail, yet so profound,
Unleashing torrents in the night,
A blaze within, where truth is found.

Radiance cuts through veils of grey,
To kindle dawn in hearts once dim,
A beacon in the break of day,
Flames of genius on a whim.

Through sudden bursts, the world revealed,
Aglow with hues of pure insight,
In every thought, a secret sealed,
Unlocks the veins of boundless light.

Ether of Invention

In the silent, unseen ether,
Where the seeds of thoughts do bloom,
Dwells the essence of endeavor,
Weaving wonders on its loom.

Gossamer threads of imagination,
Spin forth webs of grand design,
From the ether, innovation,
Manifest in syncopated time.

Invisible, yet ever near,
Source of every grand creation,
In each idea crystal clear,
Echoes whispered inspiration.

Infinite in boundless measure,
Wellspring of the human mind,
Invention's flow, our greatest treasure,
In the ether, we do find.

From the void, forms arise,
Crafted by unseen's hand,
In the ether, all resides,
Dreams and visions ever grand.

Luminescent Muse

Amidst the shadows softly falls,
A muse aglow with subtle grace,
Illuminating silent halls,
With whispers from an unseen place.

In her light, the world transforms,
Every thought a gleaming star,
Guiding hearts through tempests' storms,
Her luminescence near and far.

Ideas in her radiance bloom,
Eclipsing doubt's encroaching might,
Brighter than a sunlit room,
She births the dawn from deepest night.

In her glow, true magic thrives,
Imbued in words, in art, in song,
As if each spark within her lives,
To make creative spirits strong.

The muse of light, forever near,
Unseen yet felt in every heart,
With luminescence pure and clear,
She kindles flames that never part.

Whimsical Journeys

Through valleys green and rivers blue,
With skies that change from grey to hue,
On paths that only dreams can chart,
We wander through the realm of heart.

In forests deep where shadows play,
Where sprites and whispers dance and sway,
We chase the light beyond the trees,
A world revealed beneath the breeze.

Oceans vast with secrets old,
Echo tales in voices bold,
In ships of thought we sail afar,
Guided by a distant star.

Mountains high with peaks unseen,
Where clouds embrace the white serene,
Each step we take a story spun,
In endless quest beneath the sun.

By moonlit nights and suns that rise,
With countless dreams that greet our eyes,
Whimsical journeys shape our fate,
In realms of wonder, we create.

Dreamt into Existence

In twilight's veil, where shadows meet,
A world is born, both wild and sweet,
From thoughts that whisper in the night,
And dreams that shine with a celestial light.

Stars sew patterns in the sky,
We drift on winds of silent sigh,
Each twinkling light a dream begun,
In cosmic dance with morning's sun.

In depths of slumber, visions grow,
Crafting realms we come to know,
With every breath and flitting scene,
We build our world within the dream.

Ethereal plains where whispers sing,
Carving futures, taking wing,
Ideas weave through endless space,
In dreams, they find a sacred place.

And when we wake with morning's blush,
Dreamt into existence, in a rush,
The echoes of our night-tide quest,
Still linger in our beating breast.

Illumination's Brush

Strokes of dawn upon the sky,
Painting hues as night doth fly,
With gentle hand and subtle flare,
Illumination greets the air.

The world awakens, colors bright,
With each caress of morning light,
It shapes the hills, the trees, the streams,
Igniting life with golden beams.

In quiet corners, shadows blend,
Soft and warm, they twist and bend,
A masterpiece, each day reborn,
With every glimpse of waking morn.

Eyes wide open to the glow,
Tracing patterns high and low,
Illumination's brush reveals,
A canvas spun on nature's wheels.

And as the twilight starts to creep,
The colors fade, the world to sleep,
Each stroke of light, so carefully placed,
Tomorrow's dawn, again embraced.

Revolution of Ideas

In minds that roam through distant lands,
Ideas bloom in shifting sands,
A revolution starts to stir,
In whispers loud and thoughts that purr.

The spark of change in silent might,
Grows in strength through darkest night,
With voices raised, the silence breaks,
And new ideas the dawn awakes.

Questions posed in hearts and minds,
Challenge truths of ancient kinds,
The revolution spins its thread,
Unraveling paths that once were tread.

In words and deeds, in art's embrace,
Ideas take form and find their place,
With every step, the future drawn,
In colors bold, a world reborn.

Horizons stretch with vision clear,
Each new thought dissolves the fear,
The revolution, endless quest,
Of ideas born and put to test.

Renaissance of the Mind

In whispers of the ancient muse,
Where thoughts and dreams entwine,
A renaissance of mind imbues,
New worlds both bold and fine.

From shadows of the past we rise,
To heights unseen, unfound,
With every dawn, a fresh surprise,
In wisdom we are crowned.

Glistening trails of knowledge gleam,
Through corridors of time,
Each brush of thought, a vivid dream,
A staircase to the prime.

Inquiries spark like fireflies,
Bright constellations form,
A galaxy in human eyes,
A dance within the storm.

Let every echo ring anew,
In chambers of the mind,
For in this light, we search, pursue,
And endless truths we find.

Calligraphy of Dreams

The quill dips in a twilight hue,
Ink whispers tales untold,
On parchment skies, a dreamer's view,
Where words like stars unfold.

Each stroke a journey, woven fine,
Through realms of heart and thought,
In delicate lines, design divine,
Our dreams in ink are caught.

The moonlight spells in silver script,
A saga soft and true,
Where fantasies and wishes drift,
In calligraphy's hue.

Swirls of wonder, loops of grace,
A dance upon the scroll,
In every curve, a friend's embrace,
A language of the soul.

With every dawn, we pen anew,
Our hopes, desires, and schemes,
In artful letters, pure and true,
The calligraphy of dreams.

Brushed with Brilliance

A canvas waits in silent thrill,
For strokes of dazzling light,
As brilliance brushes bold and still,
Transforming dark to bright.

In hues of gold and sapphire blue,
The visions start to glow,
Each stroke a vivid, vibrant cue,
Where dreams and colors flow.

The artist's heart in every line,
Pulsates with rhythmic beat,
Creating forms both pure, divine,
A masterpiece complete.

With every wave of brush and hue,
A story comes to birth,
In moments glanced, a world anew,
A testament of worth.

So let us paint with passion's hand,
Our lives in vivid blend,
For in each stroke, we understand,
Creation has no end.

Poetic Inventiveness

In valleys deep, on mountains high,
Our words begin to weave,
A tapestry of thought and sky,
Beyond what we believe.

With every verse, a frontier crossed,
New realms of heart and mind,
In letters bold, where dreams are tossed,
Invention we will find.

The melody of prose and rhyme,
Sings songs of boundless flight,
In meters grand, through steps of time,
Where day embraces night.

Our pens, they dance with fervent grace,
Each line, a spark anew,
In crafted phrases, we embrace,
The genius in review.

So write we must, with hearts afire,
Each word, a blazing star,
For in this craft, we never tire,
Invention takes us far.

Whispered Inspirations

In shadows where the quiet dwells,
Ideas are like hidden wells.
A whisper calls the muse to play,
And turns the night into day.

A soft breeze brushes through the mind,
A realm where endless dreams unwind.
Paths of light and dark entwine,
In this space where thoughts resign.

Stars above in silent grace,
Guide the heart through mystic chase.
Their twinkle whispers words so sweet,
For hearts that ache with fire and heat.

In twilight's hush, the world retreats,
Leaving whispers in the sheets.
In those murmurs, deep and low,
Wisdom blooms, and insights grow.

Valleys deep and mountains high,
In whispered tones, the spirits fly.
Through silent echoes, pure and bright,
Whispered inspirations light the night.

Spectrum of Thoughts

In the palette of the mind,
Thoughts in colors they unwind.
Each hue a feeling, bold or shy,
Spreading wide across the sky.

Blue for peace and calm embrace,
Green for growth in life's sweet chase.
Red for passion, fierce and wild,
Yellow for the sun's mild smile.

Violet dreams take soothing flight,
Orange glows with pure delight.
Every shade a story told,
In silent whispers, brave and bold.

Thoughts like rainbows, swift they change,
A spectrum wide and full of range.
From dawn to dusk, they weave and wane,
Colors dance in joy and pain.

The mind, a canvas ever vast,
With thoughts, both present and past.
In this spectrum, wisdom's sought,
In every hue, a deeper thought.

Inventive Heartbeats

In the pulse of life so bright,
Beats a heart with endless might.
Ideas spring like morning dew,
In inventive heartbeats, pure and true.

Rhythms dance in moments still,
Crafting dreams with skillful will.
Each heartbeat weaves an arcane tale,
In a world where wonders sail.

In the silence, thoughts ignite,
Sparks of brilliance in the night.
From the heart, creations flow,
In whispered beats, they start to grow.

Innovation's gentle thrum,
Beckons, calls, inspiring some.
In every beat, a world anew,
Crafted fresh in each debut.

In the boundless, endless quest,
Heartbeats drive and never rest.
Innovations rise and gleam,
In each heartbeat's brilliant stream.

Envisioned Euphoria

Eyes closed, the world anew,
Dreams envisioned, bright and true.
Euphoria's gentle, soft caress,
In visions, we find sweet excess.

Floating on a thought's embrace,
Every worry, time displace.
In this realm of pure delight,
Souls take flight in endless night.

Colors swirl in joy profound,
Music, laughter all around.
The heart's desires, finally free,
In this envisioned reverie.

Hope and wonder intertwine,
In this dream, we claim as mine.
Euphoria lights the sacred way,
Where dreams dance in bright array.

In this space, our spirits soar,
Finding bliss and so much more.
Envisioned joy, eternally,
A timeless dance, forever free.

Timeless Fancies

In whispers of wind, they dance and play,
Twilight dreams where shadows sway.
Memories carved in ancient stone,
Endless horizons, journey unknown.

Eclipsing days and fleeting nights,
They sing of stars and boundless lights.
Within the heart, a secret spring,
A melody that time shall bring.

Lost in echoes of tomorrow's dawn,
Each fantasy, a story drawn.
Within these realms, the soul is free,
Timeless fancies call to thee.

Kaleidoscopic Dreams

Fragments of color swirl and spin,
A mosaic of where we've been.
Each pattern tells a tale anew,
In these dreams, we find our clue.

Embers of thought in variegated hues,
A symphony of infinite views.
Shapes and shadows, swift as light,
We chase the whispers in the night.

Through prisms sharp, yet silky soft,
We drift, we soar, we fall aloft.
In every turn a revelation gleams,
Embraced within kaleidoscopic dreams.

Genesis of Imagination

From void to vast, a spark ignites,
A genesis in boundless nights.
Images born from silent flares,
A universe within our stares.

Mind's eye awakens, weaving tales,
Upon ethereal, unseen trails.
Mountains rise and rivers flow,
In dreams, the seeds of wonder grow.

Creation's hand, unseen, divine,
Crafts realms where shadows intertwine.
Each thought a world, each dream a nation,
In this, the genesis of imagination.

Illuminated Thoughts

In the folds of dusk, where silence stays,
A lantern lights the shadowed ways.
Ideas spark in twilight's grace,
Illuminating every place.

Whispers form in quiet minds,
Carving paths that thought designs.
Bright reflections dance and glide,
In thought's embrace, they abide.

Steps taken on a luminescent path,
Chasing dreams in aftermath.
Hope, like dawn, forever sought,
Guided by illuminated thought.

Inventing Horizons

Beyond the edge of sight, a realm unplanned,
Where dreams collide with sands of time, unshaken,
Horizons stretch in hues, by heart's command,
Invention blooms where boundless thoughts awaken.

A whisper of the dawn, a gentle blaze,
Inspiration's light breaks through shadowed confines,
Where mind and spirit wander through the maze,
Creating worlds with ink and endless lines.

Rivers of ideas carve their silent trails,
Across the tapestry of morning skies,
Discovery sets sail on midnight sails,
Boundless, bound for where imagination flies.

Through realms unseen, beneath a million stars,
The pulse of possibility runs deep,
Horizons weave a tale behind closed bars,
Where dreams are birthed, and creativity leaps.

In the vast expanse, a journey begins,
A chase for what's beyond the sun's embrace,
Horizons blend, where every vision spins,
Inventing paths through time, to find a place.

Twilight of Ideas

As daylight fades, the twilight calls anew,
Where thoughts converge in evening's quiet glow,
A realm of shadows paints a subtle view,
Ideas dance in whispers, soft and slow.

The sky becomes a canvas for the mind,
Where hues of thought in endless patterns form,
In that serene, where purest dreams unwind,
And untamed creativity takes storm.

Between the dusk and dawn, innovation thrives,
In moments where the heart and soul align,
A symphony of notions gently strives,
To craft the world's next visionary line.

Soft tendrils of the night entwine with light,
Weaving dreams that only twilight knows,
In that embrace, thoughts take their soaring flight,
To realms where endless inspiration flows.

The twilight births a universe within,
Ideas blend with the stars' eternal gleam,
In that tender dusk, new worlds begin,
Where the night cradles the most profound dream.

Sculpting Daydreams

In the quiet lulls of passing noon,
Where daydreams mold like clay in idle minds,
A realm unfurls beneath the sunlit moon,
Where sculptors of imagination find.

With gentle hands, they shape the fleeting mist,
Crafting visions from the remnants of thought,
Each whispering breeze a muse they can't resist,
To form the unseen worlds that dreams have brought.

With eyes half-closed, in reverie's embrace,
They carve out tales from shadows, light, and air,
A dance of wonder in a secret space,
Where every glance reveals a canvas rare.

In sculpted dreams, the world begins anew,
A place where boundless fantasies unfold,
In every line, a novel point of view,
Each stroke a testament to tales retold.

So let them dream, these artisans of mind,
For in their craft, the world finds fresh designs,
In every daydream, futures redefined,
Sculpting realms where endless beauty shines.

Innovation's Melody

In the quiet hum of morning light,
A melody of thoughts begins to play,
Innovation stirs from silent night,
Composing every dawn with each new day.

With every note, a notion takes its form,
Ideas blend in harmony and grace,
Chords of brilliance rise, their warmth transform,
The world reshaped in symphonies' embrace.

The rhythm of the heart beats pure and true,
Guiding minds through endless woven themes,
A song of progress swells in skies of blue,
Where melodies give life to dreams and schemes.

Invention sings in bridges yet unmade,
Each chorus builds on breakthrough's gentle might,
Creating pathways, through the dusk and shade,
Illuminating future with its light.

So listen close, to Innovation's theme,
A soundtrack to the world yet to unfold,
In every note, a fragment of a dream,
In melodies of creation, stories told.

Infinite Variations

In twilight's serene embrace, we find,
A symphony of colors intertwined,
Whispering breezes blend and play,
Infinite variations, night and day.

Stars that shimmer in boundless skies,
Reflect endless dreams in our eyes,
Patterns shift, a dance without end,
Universe's beauty, our hearts defend.

Mountains loom with ancient grace,
Timeless wonders etched on space,
Rivers carve their winding trails,
In nature's book, countless tales.

Every leaf a story told,
With hues transforming, bold,
Nature whispers soft refrains,
Infinite variations in life's veins.

Embrace the flux, the endless change,
In their mystery, re-arrange,
Paths uncharted, futures bright,
Infinite variations, infinite light.

Imaginative Resonance

Echoes of thoughts in the mind's deep well,
Creativity casts its vibrant spell,
Images blend and swiftly rise,
Imaginative resonance, in disguise.

Dreams take flight on wings of gold,
Stories in colors, brave and bold,
Unseen realms in daylight's gleam,
Where fantasy and reality seem.

In quiet moments, seeds are sown,
Ideas and visions all our own,
Voices whisper, soft but clear,
Within us, inspiration, ever near.

Songs of wonder, melodies free,
Imagination's vast, boundless sea,
Through every chord, in every note,
Imaginative resonance, poets wrote.

Dance of thoughts in creative stream,
Reality and dream, we seamlessly seam,
Beyond the stars, through endless space,
Imaginative resonance, our minds embrace.

Visionary Streams

Rivers of light in the mind's terrain,
Flowing through valleys, hills, and plain,
Thoughts converge, like crystal beams,
In the heart of visionary streams.

Mountains high with vistas wide,
Knowledge woven in every stride,
Each peak a new horizon gleams,
A journey forged in visionary streams.

Forests dense with whispers old,
Where secrets of the world unfold,
Pathways twist in moonlit dreams,
Magic courses through visionary streams.

Oceans vast, in deep repose,
Holding truths that no one knows,
Waves that crash with silent screams,
Wisdom flows in visionary streams.

We sail on ships of hopes untamed,
Futures traced and unclaimed,
In the dawn's ethereal gleams,
We find ourselves in visionary streams.

Innovative Labyrinth

Within the maze of thoughts we walk,
Innovation's voice begins to talk,
Each turn reveals a hidden clue,
Innovative labyrinth, always new.

Walls of ideas, corridors bright,
Guiding us with insight's light,
Every step a bold endeavor,
Paths that twist and turn forever.

Behind each door, a world awaits,
Bound by neither time nor fates,
Solutions weave like silk of dreams,
In the innovative labyrinth's schemes.

Infinite routes to where we go,
Boundless realms we come to know,
Creation whispers, then it screams,
Through the labyrinth's complex themes.

Lose ourselves, yet find anew,
Inspiration's touch, refreshing dew,
In the heart of thought streams,
Lives the innovative labyrinth's beams.

Spark of Genius

In quiet moments, thoughts ignite,
A burst of brilliance, pure and bright.
Through shadows cast by doubt and fear,
The spark of genius now draws near.

An idea blooms, a seed of light,
To challenge day, transform the night.
Unseen paths, clear to those who dare,
The spark of genius whispers there.

From mind to hand, the journey slow,
Yet in this spark, dreams start to grow.
A flame within, it cannot die,
The spark of genius lights the sky.

Across the canvas, pure and wide,
New worlds emerge, truths cannot hide.
With every stroke, the heart reveals,
The spark of genius, what it feels.

A dance of thoughts, a brilliant show,
In every mind, the seeds can grow.
With courage fed, ambitions fly,
The spark of genius reaches high.

Crafting Daydreams

Eyes half-closed, yet visions clear,
Imagination draws them near.
In every whisper, scenes unfold,
Crafting daydreams, stories told.

Fields of wonder, skies so deep,
In these dreams, our fears we keep.
Through winding roads, and hidden streams,
Crafting daydreams, chasing gleams.

The colors blend in hues unseen,
Worlds where every heart is keen.
From mundane life, we briefly part,
Crafting daydreams, filling heart.

Each dream a tale yet to commence,
Filled with magic, woven sense.
With every breath, the visions wean,
Crafting daydreams, serene.

Infinite realms where none refrain,
In dreams, we dance, released from chain.
Through vivid lands and cosmic seams,
Crafting daydreams, endless themes.

Mind's Odyssey

Through endless stars, the mind does trek,
In cosmic wonders, paths it flecks.
A voyage endless, rich and free,
Embarked upon, mind's odyssey.

The realms unknown, we yearn to find,
With courage fed and fate behind.
Just close your eyes and cast your plea,
The doors will part in mind's odyssey.

Each thought a beacon, guiding true,
Exploring realms beyond our view.
In whispers soft, and visions flee,
We journey forth in mind's odyssey.

Across the void and through the mist,
Each idea turns to a twist.
New wonders felt so vibrantly,
In every step of mind's odyssey.

The place where dream and truth collide,
In realms where time and space subside.
From start to end, we are but free,
Forever bound to mind's odyssey.

Wings of Creativity

With open heart and vision wide,
We set upon imagination's tide.
With colors, sounds, and untold grace,
Wings of creativity embrace.

Through artful skies where we can soar,
Each thought a feather, dreams restore.
In realms where limits cease to be,
Wings of creativity set free.

From ink to voice, from clay to song,
In every form, we do belong.
Unleashing thoughts, our spirits see,
The world anew, with wings of creativity.

No chains to bind, no walls confine,
In endless worlds where we design.
A journey shared, a mind so free,
Ignited by, those wings of creativity.

In every heart, the ember burns,
For every soul, the moment yearns.
Reach out, create, and let us be,
Raised high aloft, on wings of creativity.

Labyrinth of Ideas

Twists and turns within the mind,
Paths to knowledge, hard to find,
Creativity's endless sprawl,
Echoes in each hidden hall.

Wandering through thought's terrain,
Epiphany both joy and pain,
Questions linger, shadows cast,
In this maze of present, past.

Walls adorned with wild dreams,
Flowing like the winding streams,
Each corridor, a mystery,
Tracing steps of history.

In the silence, answers gleam,
Threads of truth, a golden seam,
Every corner, insight's spark,
Guiding lights when all is dark.

Labyrinth where thoughts reside,
Journey inward, deep inside,
Mapless, endless, bound to roam,
Seeking wisdom, finding home.

Prism of Possibilities

Light refracted, dreams dispersed,
Infinite, the universe,
Many facets, stories told,
Through the prism, futures fold.

Colors burst in radiant hues,
Choices vast as morning dews,
Hope, ambition, love, and strife,
Each one carving paths through life.

In the spectrum, life is seen,
Every shade, a nameless dream,
Possibilities, boundless sea,
Charting courses, wild and free.

Reflections dance on mirrored streams,
Whispers of forgotten dreams,
Possibilities await,
Hearts embraced by endless fate.

Through this prism, visions blend,
Prisms where all roads ascend,
In its glow, the paths align,
Endless choices, all divine.

Boundless Horizons

On the edge of endless skies,
Beyond the known, where hopes arise,
Horizons stretch, forever wide,
Paths unmarked, where dreams abide.

Journey forth, the world unfolds,
Every step, a story told,
Mountains rise and waters gleam,
Boundless as the endless dream.

Whispers on the winds we hear,
Promises both bright and clear,
Stars that guide and suns that set,
Boundless horizons never met.

Endless ocean, sky, and land,
Possibilities, unplanned,
Horizons call with siren's song,
To realms where we have yet to belong.

Boundless realms, where hearts may soar,
Limitless, forevermore,
Horizons beckon, futures bright,
To endless days and endless night.

Palette of Wonder

Brushstrokes on a canvas wide,
Colors blend, where dreams reside,
Palette bright with every shade,
In each hue, wonder displayed.

Vivid valleys, skies of blue,
Mountains rise in pastel view,
In this spectrum, hearts delight,
Every tint, a burst of light.

Crimson dawns and twilight gold,
Stories painted, futures told,
Every stroke, a whispered sigh,
Wonders gleam before our eye.

Nature's hues and crafted skill,
Blend in portraits, never still,
Palette rich with endless flair,
Wonders painted everywhere.

In each color, life is found,
Every tone, a joyful sound,
Palette wide, where dreams take flight,
In the colors, pure delight.

Garden of Ideas

In a garden lush with bloom,
Thoughts emerge from fertile ground,
Petals whisper in the room,
Silent musings all around.

Every raindrop, a new spark,
Nourishing the seeds of thought,
Dreams take vision in the dark,
From the soil, wisdom's caught.

Ideas rise like morning sun,
Casting shadows of insight,
Each begins but never's done,
Growing strong after the night.

Paths of query gently tread,
Through the rows of concept green,
Lush and full the mind's own bed,
Fertile with each verdant scene.

In this garden minds shall play,
Tending sprout and coiled vine,
Ever bright the dawning day,
In the garden thoughts entwine.

Strokes of Wonder

In each stroke, a world does lie,
Colors blend in harmony,
Brushes dance, the canvas sigh,
Captured moments wild and free.

Light and shadow, dark and bright,
Weave together, hue on hue,
Strokes of wonder in the night,
Paint a tale both old and new.

Every paint drip tells a story,
Not a word can match its grace,
Nature's beauty, human glory,
Comes to life in this embrace.

Lines that bend and shapes that sway,
Form a scene that eyes adore,
Lives connected in display,
Masterpieces to explore.

In each splash, potential flows,
Art becomes a boundless sea,
Where the boundless spirit goes,
Free in strokes of mystery.

Symphony of the Mind

Thoughts in harmony combine,
Lighting up the darkened void,
Notes of reason sweetly chime,
Through the pathways they've employed.

Silent music, loud and clear,
Waves of introspection feed,
Nothing distant, nothing near,
Truths that every mind shall need.

Mind and heart in chorus sing,
Words that bloom and never wilt,
Contours deftly drawn in ring,
Crafting moments strongly built.

On the stage of memory wide,
Symphonies of wonder play,
Every thought a gentle guide,
Leading onward through the day.

Listen close to wisdom's tune,
Echoing in chambers deep,
Symphony beneath the moon,
In our minds forever keep.

Infinite the melody,
Played upon the strings of thought,
Whispered in eternity,
In each mind the song is caught.

Visionary Valleys

Beyond the peaks of doubting fear,
Lies the valley's vast domain,
Visionaries bold appear,
Dreaming dreams through joy and pain.

Whispers of the future's gleam,
Ripple through the crystal air,
Ideas flow like steady stream,
Minds unbound and hearts laid bare.

Paths unknown explored with zest,
Every turn a new delight,
In these valleys, thoughts find rest,
Glistening in the morning light.

Bridges spanning chasms wide,
Built with fragments of the soul,
In these valleys, free to glide,
Insight flowing, making whole.

Visionaries rise and fall,
But their echoes ever stay,
In these valleys, one and all,
Forge the light to guide the way.

Fields of Inspiration

In fields where dreams do gently sway,
The muse is found in light and play.
A whisper through the golden air,
Inspires the soul to climb and dare.

Where thoughts are seeds, in fertile ground,
New visions sprout without a sound.
The heart's own landscape, vast and wide,
Creates a path where hope can bide.

Beneath the azure, endless skies,
Imagination's echoes rise.
They tell of stories yet untold,
Of courage bright, and hearts so bold.

Among the poppies' scarlet gleam,
Lie endless hues of life's grand scheme.
For in these fields, our spirits find,
The boundless flights of open mind.

So wander here, where dreams unfold,
In realms of green and marigold.
For in these fields of pure delight,
We capture stardust in the night.

Echoes of Innovation

In clockwork gears and circuits bright,
Innovation takes its flight.
From whispers of the curious mind,
New worlds and wonders we do find.

The echo of a bold design,
Transforms the essence of our time.
From ancient lore to future's crest,
Imagination never rests.

Through binary and quantum leaps,
A dawning comprehension seeps.
In labs and lofts where minds convene,
New paradigms are built, unseen.

The fabric of our dreams attained,
From thoughts that never were constrained.
Across the ages, pure and clear,
These echoes drive us year to year.

With every spark, a universe,
A multitude of dreams diverse.
The echoes of our questing minds,
Leave legacies for all mankind.

Mind's Odyssey

Into the deep, where thoughts arise,
The questing mind, unbounded, flies.
Across the realms of time and space,
In search of wisdom's sacred grace.

A voyage through the silent veil,
Where whispers of the cosmos hail.
Each notion like a guiding star,
Leads deeper into realms afar.

Through labyrinths of light and night,
The seeker's heart is pure and bright.
With every step, a mystery,
Unlocks itself in majesty.

Beyond the edge of what we know,
New insights like a river flow.
In seas of thought, unmapped, unseen,
The odyssey of mind's serene.

Return to shores of waking day,
With treasures that the heart convey.
For journeys in the mind's expanse,
Bring forth the light in every glance.

Fantasia Unleashed

In realms where wildest dreams unfold,
Imagination's tales are told.
A symphony of sights and sounds,
In Fantasia, there are no bounds.

Where dragons soar and fairies glide,
And myths and legends freely bide.
Each fantasy a truth reveals,
In magic's realm, the heart soon heals.

Through forests deep and mountains high,
The soul is given wings to fly.
In colors bright and shadows deep,
The specters of our passions leap.

Unleashed from chains of daily grind,
Fantasia frees the caged mind.
With every thought, new worlds are born,
In waking dreams and twilight morn.

So dare to dream, and venture forth,
Explore each story's endless worth.
In realms of fantasy and light,
Find endless joy in boundless flight.

Mind's Palette

The canvas waits with bated breath,
For colors yet to find their path,
Imagination paints its quest,
Beyond the bounds of time's math.

Shades blend in a mystic dance,
Ideas bloom, then fade away,
Each stroke given a fleeting chance,
To capture dawn or end of day.

Thoughts in amber, hues in blue,
Weaving tales untold, unseen,
Vivid visions breaking through,
The mind's palette: bold, serene.

Each new layer tells a story,
Hidden deep within the mind,
Capturing both pain and glory,
Leaving mundane life behind.

Creation flows, a current swift,
From heart to hand it does impart,
A masterpiece as thoughts uplift,
The boundless palette of the heart.

Artistic Odyssey

Voyage through realms of boundless art,
Where every sight a wonder brings,
Across a sea where dreams do start,
With brush and quill, on spirit's wings.

Echoes of an ancient muse,
Whisper guidance in the night,
Through labyrinths of every hue,
Creating worlds by candlelight.

In halls of gold and silver thread,
Imagination roams so free,
Through shades of violet, blues, and red,
A timeless, endless odyssey.

Each creation sparks anew,
Unfolding stories yet untold,
With every shade and every hue,
A history of hearts grown bold.

So journey on, dear voyager,
Through landscapes vast and thoughts so deep,
For in this artistic odyssey,
Your soul its truest art shall keep.

Inkwell of Dreams

Dip your quill in inkwell deep,
A reservoir of boundless dreams,
Where hopes and whispers softly seep,
Forming worlds of moonlit streams.

Words unfurl like petals new,
On pages pure, yet to be stained,
Scribing thoughts both old and true,
Through shadows cast and light regained.

In the stillness, hearts confide,
Secret yearnings, silent pleas,
Through the lines, the pen does glide,
Weaving tales on twilight's breeze.

Wisps of wonder, flicks of fate,
Etched in ink, both swift and bold,
In this never-ending state,
Stories penned, and dreams unfold.

The inkwell of dreams overflows,
With every stroke, it breathes anew,
A testament to hearts that know,
The power held in words so true.

Dreamt in Color

In silent nights where colors bloom,
A tapestry of dreams unfurls,
Vivid visions pierce the gloom,
In this dreamscape, boundless swirls.

Emerald meadows stretch afar,
Golden suns and azure skies,
Every hue, a guiding star,
Dreamt in color, no disguise.

Through the spectrum, wander free,
Lost in worlds where limits fade,
Crafting futures yet to be,
With every stroke, each hue portrayed.

Crimson passions, gentle greens,
Merge to form a rainbow's arc,
In these dreamt in color scenes,
Every shade ignites a spark.

As dawn approaches, dreams may scatter,
Yet their hues in memory stay,
Dreamt in color, mind's laughter,
Painting life in every way.

Crafted Realities

In fields where dreams converge and blend,
We sculpt the worlds that never end,
With hands of hope and minds so vast,
We shape the future from the past.

Ideas dance like radiant beams,
In twilight's glow, we build our dreams,
From scattered thoughts to solid forms,
Our crafted realities transform.

Each brick, a whisper in the night,
Each stone, a wish for morning light,
We forge with love, we dream with care,
In realms where hearts and hands repair.

A tapestry of time and space,
Where every thread reveals a face,
These crafted realms where spirits play,
Are born anew with each new day.

Dreamweaver's Workshop

In the heart of starlit skies,
Where moon and dreams and magic rise,
A workshop blooms with endless light,
The Dreamweaver spins her flight.

Threads of silver, webs of gold,
Stories waiting to be told,
With every touch, a new design,
In worlds where endless wonders shine.

Her loom of thought, her spindle bright,
Weaves the fabric of the night,
She chases shadows, blends their lore,
Turns ordinary into more.

In corners dark, where visions sleep,
She plucks them from the silent deep,
Crafting dreams with tender hands,
The Dreamweaver's art commands.

Boundless Envisioning

In realms where limits cease to bind,
We journey through the endless mind,
Where thoughts unfurl like blooms in spring,
And boundless dreams take wing.

The skies, an infinite expanse,
Invite our hearts to dream and dance,
With every breath, a vision clear,
The future's path, our frontier.

A canvas wide, a palette grand,
We paint with hope, we build, we stand,
In boundless space, our spirits soar,
Envisioning forevermore.

Each star, a guide, each dawn, a call,
To push beyond the known and small,
In every heart, a spark, a flame,
Of boundless dreams, we lay our claim.

Inspiration's Muse

Upon her wings of thoughts, I glide,
Through fields where endless dreams reside,
Her whispers light, her touch a spark,
That ignites the flame within the dark.

The Muse of Inspiration's song,
Carries me on winds so strong,
She breathes in me the fire to write,
With strokes of brilliance, pure and bright.

In caverns deep, where shadows reign,
She pulls me up through night and pain,
Her guiding voice, a beacon true,
That leads me to a world anew.

With every verse, her spirit flows,
In every line, her essence grows,
Inspiration's Muse, forever near,
Turns silence into songs we hear.

Whispers of Imagination

In silent dreams, where shadows play,
Beyond the realms of night and day.
A whisper tells of lands untold,
Where tales of wonder unfold.

In meadows kissed by twilight's gleam,
The rivers dance, in moon's soft beam.
Each star a muse, a story spun,
In a world where all are one.

Mountains high and valleys deep,
Guard secrets that the ages keep.
With every whisper, visions soar,
Imagination's boundless lore.

Castles rise in clouds of gold,
Heroes brave, and hearts of bold.
In silent whispers, magic streams,
Waking life from hidden dreams.

Oceans vast and forest dense,
All awake in sensing tense.
For whispers of imagination,
Invoke waves of fascination.

Symphony of Colors

Brushed by dawn's ethereal touch,
Shades of gold, an artist's clutch.
Morning blooms with hues so bright,
In a symphony of light.

The forest hums in green embrace,
Nature's palette, strokes with grace.
Emerald leaves in soft milieu,
Sing the songs of morning dew.

Twilight sets the sky on fire,
With crimson waves and golden spire.
Colors blend in twilight's kiss,
An evening's tender bliss.

Night descends in indigo,
Stars like sequins, shimmering flow.
A midnight dance of silver beams,
Coloring the land of dreams.

In every drop, a spectrum gleams,
In quiet streams, in vibrant schemes.
A symphony in colors spun,
A masterpiece by day is done.

Tapestry of Thoughts

Threads of gold and strands of grey,
Woven tales from night to day.
Mind's loom spins a web so vast,
Capturing echoes of the past.

Whispers born from ancient lore,
Ideas lost on distant shore.
Each thread tells a tale unspun,
A symphony of thoughts begun.

In quiet nooks of solitude,
Thoughts converge in interlude.
Weaving dreams with silent hands,
Creating worlds no eye understands.

Patterns form in mind's embrace,
Connections found in time and space.
A tapestry with colors rare,
Of dreams and thoughts beyond compare.

With every thought, a thread is sewn,
In elaboration's grand cologne.
A tapestry of thoughts, complete,
In the quiet mind's retreat.

Canvas of Whimsy

A stroke of chaos, colors wild,
The universe through eyes of child.
In each splash, a wish, a dream,
On a canvas where whimsies gleam.

Glimmers of a world unknown,
On unseen paths, the heart is thrown.
The canvas sings in hues bizarre,
Of flights of fancy, near and far.

Figures dance in colors bold,
With stories that are cradled, told.
Each twist and turn, a playful jest,
Whimsy's heart beats in the chest.

Splatterings of joy and woe,
In vibrant streams, emotions flow.
The canvas thrives on wild delight,
Where logic yields to endless flight.

A canvas pure, unbridled, free,
Whimsical from A to Z.
A masterpiece by heart's decree,
Where every stroke spells fantasy.

Inventive Waves

In seas of dreams, ideas flow,
Where tides of thought forever glow,
Each ripple whispers tales untold,
In waves of wonder, minds unfold.

Currents dance with endless grace,
In every crest, new hopes embrace,
Through stormy nights and sunny days,
Inventive waves carve out new ways.

With every surge, a passion ignites,
Glistening in the moon's soft lights,
Creative spirits rise and dive,
For in these waves, ideas thrive.

Horizons broad span beyond,
In ocean's heart, the dreams bond,
Innovations ebb and sway,
On inventive waves we lay.

Musing Mountains

Beneath the ancient peaks so high,
Thoughts soar as eagles in the sky,
Each stone and brook whispers then,
Secrets of the earth and men.

In shadows cast by mighty heights,
The mind ascends to boundless flights,
Every summit, a new view,
Musing mountains guide us through.

Silent sentinels, wise and grand,
Their vastness hard to understand,
Yet in their quiet, voices speak,
Of strength found in a path unique.

From base to top, the journey's long,
Through hardships met, we grow strong,
Musing mountains, guardians tall,
In their embrace, dreams enthrall.

Sparkling Vision

Glimmers dance in morning's light,
Illuminating dreams so bright,
In each sparkle, worlds unfold,
Tales of wonder yet untold.

Eyes alight with visions clear,
Blueprints of a future near,
Imagination's vivid art,
Sparkling visions, world apart.

Crystals of thought refract and gleam,
From waking hours to realms of dream,
As prisms cast a spectrum wide,
Possibilities to be tried.

From scattered stars to radiant beam,
Innovations rise to theme,
In sparkling vision, paths align,
Destinies in brilliance shine.

Garden of Genius

In fertile ground of hopeful care,
Ideas bloom in climate fair,
Each petal, thought, a radiant hue,
In the garden of genius, ever new.

Seeds of wisdom, deeply sown,
In light of knowledge, fully grown,
Tended with the hands of time,
Their blossoms reach, and oft they climb.

Where nature meets the mind's bright eye,
Creativity can amplify,
In varied forms, both wild and tame,
The garden flourishes with acclaim.

Paths of insight, winding through,
Encouraging each thought to accrue,
In the garden where brilliance breeds,
Genius thrives and beauty leads.

Realm of Whimsy

In a meadow of dreams where unicorns graze,
Fairies dance in a soft, moonlit haze.
Mushroom homes with doors so small,
Welcoming creatures, great and small.

Treetop ladders extend to the skies,
Pixies flutter with twinkling eyes.
Magic whispers through the breeze,
Enchanting all that it sees.

Rivers sparkle with liquid light,
Glimmering underwater sight.
Mermaids sing in melodious tune,
Underneath the silver moon.

Castles built of sugar and lace,
Djinns and elves share the space.
In a land where time stands still,
Endless stories, endless thrill.

Sky-painted canvases shift and gleam,
Every shade from a rainbow dream.
A place where imagination runs free,
Welcome to the Realm of Whimsy.

Fire of Innovation

From ashes rise ideas bold and bright,
Sparks of genius, a luminous sight.
Thoughts ignite in a chain reaction,
Forging the path to satisfaction.

Crafting visions with detailed care,
Dreams take shape in heated air.
Man and mind in fervent dance,
An ever-evolving, daring romance.

Invention's glow lights the night,
Casting shadows, chasing fright.
Curiosity fuels the blaze,
Leading through the darkest maze.

Hammers strike with rhythmic glee,
Molten dreams yearn to break free.
Blueprints drawn with passion's fire,
Scaling peaks of higher desire.

Embodied in creative flame,
Burns a quest none can tame.
Boldly stride with fervent pace,
Innovation's fire, a boundless space.

Cultivating Wonder

In the heart of autumn's gold,
Seeds of marvel slowly unfold.
Glimpses of the unseen and grand,
Nurtured by a gentle hand.

Raindrops chime on silent ground,
Wonders waiting to be found.
Mysteries bloom in gardened plots,
Nurseries of curious thoughts.

Through the lens of morning dew,
Worlds reveal a vibrant hue.
Enigmas grow beneath the sun,
In fields where imagination runs.

A tender touch on fragile leaves,
Fosters what the soul believes.
Whispers of the unknown weave,
A tapestry of webs they cleave.

Cherish each and every sprout,
Wonder thrives when given clout.
Tend the roots, let magic rise,
Cultivation in joyful eyes.

Epiphany's Embrace

Sudden burst of blinding light,
Clearing fog from mental sight.
Ideas blossom, take their place,
In the warmth of epiphany's embrace.

Truths emerge from shadowed nooks,
Inspired by forgotten books.
Insight weaves through tangled threads,
Weaving clarity where it treads.

Moments paused in whispered time,
Echoes of a silent chime.
Thoughts align and take their cue,
To paint the mind in coherent hue.

Revelation's gentle kiss,
Leaves no thought amiss.
Miracles in the space confined,
Limitless within the mind.

Hold these sparks with tender care,
For they are fleeting, rare.
Epiphany's embrace, a sacred rite,
Guiding through the endless night.